This is what
I look like.

THIS IS HOW
I DO IT

This is
my name.

& MATT LAMOTHE

THANK YOU!

This project required an incredible amount of help from various relatives, friends, and friends' relatives who contributed their time and effort to find kids for this book. Thanks to you all, and especially to the parents of the kids who agreed to participate.

I would also like to thank Anna Rosling Rönnlund for creating the Dollar Street project (www.gapminder.org/dollar-street) and to the amazing photographers listed below for allowing their work to be used to help educate others about the way people live throughout the globe:

PHOTOGRAPHY CREDITS *(for Dollar Street)*

Johan Eriksson: Manirapasha (This is me), Romina (This is my pet), Keza (This is my pet + family photo)

Yrsa Kleijkers: Maral (This is me + family photo)

Moa Karlberg: Ida (This is me), Prathana (This is where I live)

Zoriah Miller: Kevin (This is me), Franklin (This is what I see out of my window), Zakaria (This is how I get around), Chiyembekezo (This is what I eat for lunch), Karim (This is how we cook our food), Maclean, Macdecide & Maxmillan (This is how we cook our food)

Jonathan Taylor: Tanaporn (This is who I live with), Lurongdeji (This is how I get around + family photo)

Gmb Akash: Bindurani (This is who I live with)

Eman Jomaa: Mohammed (This is my pet)

Luc Forsyth: Carlo (This is where I live + family photo), Kong Darung (This is how we cook our food), Susadh (This is where I live), The Hossains (This is how I get around)

Alisa Sidorenko: The Kudryashovs (This is where I live)

Konstatins Sigulis: Roberts (This is how I get around)

Victrixia Montes: Xali (This is what I eat for lunch)

Aleksander Schoeffel: Helena (This is how we cook our food)

And of course, a huge thank you to my editor, Ariel Richardson, for her creative insight, and the team at Chronicle for their dedication to quality and attention to detail.

ISBN 978-1-4521-7460-0

Manufactured by Vivar Printing, Selangor Darul Ehsan, Malaysia, in June 2019.

Design by Jenny Volvovski.
Art direction by Alice Seiler.

Typeset in New Century Schoolbook and Brandon Grotesque.
The illustrations in this book were rendered digitally.

10 9 8 7 6 5 4 3 2 1

Chronicle Books LLC
680 Second Street
San Francisco, California 94107

Chronicle Books—we see things differently. Become part of our community at www.chroniclekids.com.

Distributed in Europe by
Abrams & Chronicle Books Ltd.
1 West Smithfield, 1st Floor
London EC1A 9JU

Levi, from the Netherlands, wakes up in his own room on a bed that used to belong to his uncle when he was a child. He covers himself with a comforter, but removes the filling in the summer so it's not too warm.

THIS IS HOW I DO IT

MATT LAMOTHE

One Day in
the Life of You
and 59 Real Kids
from Around
the World

chronicle books · san francisco

MONGOLIA
Maral is seven years old.

SWEDEN
Ida is ten years old.

BOLIVIA
Kevin is six years old.

RWANDA
Manirapasha is thirteen years old.

This is me.

My name is _Aiden   Gangahan_.

I am ___6___ years old.

H ℓ ıı O

I write in the _____ English _____ language.

你好

CHINA
"Ni hao" is "Hello"
in Chinese.

Jambo

KENYA
"Jambo" is "Hello"
in Swahili.

Привіт

UKRAINE
"Pryvit" is "Hello"
in Ukrainian.

ISRAEL
"Shalom" is "Hello"
in Hebrew. It is written
from right to left.

ETHIOPIA
"Iwi selami newi" is
"Hello" in Amharic.

IRAQ
"Assalam Alaikum" is
a typical greeting in
Arabic. It means "Peace
be upon you."

GREECE
"Chairete" is "Hello"
in Greek.

PERU
Neyser lives with his mom, Sofía, his dad, Isaías, his brothers, Ribaldo and Eber, and his little sister, Neida. He also has four older siblings who don't live with them.

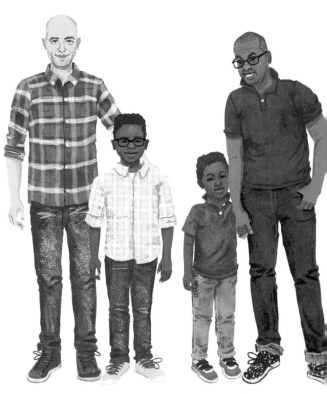

UNITED STATES
Simon lives with his dad, Rumaan, his dad, David, and his younger brother, Xavier.

BANGLADESH
Bindurani lives with his mom, Sabatrirani, his brother, Lochon, and his younger sister, Uttam.

THAILAND
Tanaporn lives with his grandmother, Nangmani, his grandfather, Lamai, and his older sister, Ponapat.

This is who I live with.

I live with _Mammr_____ Eddie. daddy. Aunt_
_Little Sister Sasha_____ .

This is my pet.

~~I have a pet~~ I wish I had a cat.

~~It's name is~~ _____ .

PAPUA NEW GUINEA

Romina and her family raise pigs on their farm.

PALESTINE

Mohammed has a black and white cat that he pets every day.

UNITED STATES

Audrey takes care of a light blue parakeet named Jewel.

RWANDA

Keza has a pet bunny that she shares with her two cousins, aunt, and uncle, with whom she lives.

PHILIPPINES
Carlo lives in a house built with the help of family and friends, on the outskirts of Tacloban.

KAZAKHSTAN
The Kudryashov family has lived in this six-story apartment building in Northern Kazakhstan for the past twenty-one years.

TANZANIA
Prathana lives in a two-bedroom house provided by the university where her father works, in the port city of Dar es Salaam.

NEPAL
Susadh and his parents live in a five-bedroom house in the capital city of Kathmandu.

RUSSIA

When Oleg goes to school he's required to wear a black suit, white shirt, and tie, but he gets to pick out the socks.

INDIA

When not in school, Navya typically wears a T-shirt and *lehenga* (a long skirt that covers her slippers). This one was a birthday gift from a friend.

FIJI

Sairusi wears a *sulu* (a wrap-around skirt), a patterned button-up shirt, and an undershirt, which are both tucked in. He typically goes barefoot.

BOLIVIA

When Franklin and his siblings look out their window, they see where the sprawling city of La Paz meets the snow-covered mountains.

FRANCE

From the second-floor window of his home in Strasbourg, Noah can see his vegetable garden, St. Paul's Church of Koenigshoffen, and a Jewish cemetery.

This is where I live.

I live in a(n) ____4____ Bedroom House ____,

in a city called ____East Sheen____,

in the country of ____England____.

This is what I see out of my window.

I can see _____ MY _____ Garden _____,

and hear _____ Birds _____ from my window.

This is what I wear.

I typically wear _____

_____ .

This is what I eat for breakfast.

I usually eat _____

_____ and drink _____.

MEXICO

Meli Jaune eats scrambled eggs with chard topped with *jocoque* (yogurt cheese), a side of beans, *nopales* (cactus), tomato salsa, and quesadillas. She drinks a cacao *atole* (hot milk and water thickened with corn).

SOUTH KOREA

Gayoon eats rice with beef and eggs pickled in soy sauce, seafood soup and sautéed ferns, and has water to drink.

GREAT BRITAIN

Sienna eats a malt loaf (a kind of sweet bread) and a slice of melon, and drinks a glass of milk. She also takes vitamins.

BURKINA FASO

Zakaria and his brothers' favorite way to get around is by bicycle. His family also owns a motorcycle.

LATVIA

Roberts's parents drive a red van to get to town from their family farm, where they raise goats and chickens.

CHINA

Lurongdeji lives with his mom and grandmother, who are both farmers. They use a modified motorcycle to get around.

BANGLADESH

The Hossain family owns a rickshaw. Mohammed, the father, drives it for a living, and one day dreams of buying a brand-new one.

This is how I get around.

I use _____ if I am going somewhere close,

and _____ to travel far.

This is where I learn.

There are _____ students in my class.

I learn _____,

and my favorite subject is _____.

FIJI

In Ruci's class of thirty students, girls wear blue dresses and boys wear white shirts with *sulus*. They study math, English, Fijian, social studies, science, and healthy living. For sports, they play rugby and netball.

JAPAN

Kei and her classmates wear white indoor slippers and are in charge of cleaning their classroom every day. They study ethics as well as math, science, and Japanese.

TANZANIA
Joseph calls his teacher
"Madame Becky." She's been
teaching for nine years.

UNITED STATES
Blythe calls his teacher
"Ms. Newsom." She's been
teaching for eleven years.

PERU
Ribaldo calls his teacher
"Professor Pedro." He's been
teaching for twenty-six years.

URUGUAY
Karen calls her teacher "Maestra
Marianela." She's been teaching
for over twenty years.

This is my teacher.

I call my teacher _____.

They've been teaching for _____ years.

This is what I eat for lunch.

I usually eat _____

_____ and drink _____.

I use _____ as my utensils.

VIETNAM

Xá Lị has scrambled eggs with river spinach and rice, and water to drink. She uses chopsticks to eat.

GERMANY

Charlotte has fried ground beef with potatoes and cucumber salad, and water to drink. She eats with a knife and fork.

BRAZIL

Mariana has ground beef with carrots and corn, rice, potatoes and quail eggs, and orange juice to drink. She eats with a spoon and fork.

MALAWI

Chiyembekezo has *nsima* (a thick paste made of cornmeal and water, formed into pancakes) and boiled leafy greens, and water to drink. He eats with his hands.

**THIS IS A FRUIT OR VEGETABLE
THAT GROWS NEAR ME.**

_____
is a common fruit or
vegetable where I live.

INDONESIA

Salak, also called snake
fruit, is a popular snack
in Indonesia. It's eaten by
peeling off the scaly exterior
that resembles snake skin.

PERU

Oca, grown in the Andes
region, is a tuber that
tastes like a lemony potato.
It comes in a variety of
different colors.

ANGOLA

Kiwano, also called a horned melon or African horned cucumber, is native to Sub-Saharan Africa. The slimy green interior tastes like cucumbers, but gets sweeter and sweeter as it ripens.

IRELAND

Dulse is a red seaweed that grows on the northern coasts of the Atlantic and Arctic Oceans. On the west coast of Ireland, it's dried and eaten as a snack.

MEXICO

Nopales, or prickly pear cacti, are grown throughout Mexico. After cleaning off the spines, they are eaten either raw or cooked.

NORWAY

Cloudberries grow in swampy areas in cooler Arctic climates. They are not farmed, and can only be hand-picked in the wild.

MALAYSIA

Rambutan is a tropical fruit cultivated in Southeast Asia. Its name comes from the word "rambut," which means "hair" in Malay.

IRAN
Kian goes horseback riding with his friends at a nearby stable.

RWANDA
Twice a week, Ryan and Darlene's father takes them swimming at the hotel pool.

This is how I play.

I play _____

with _____ in the _____.

This is how I help.

I help out by _____

_____.

RUSSIA
Anton, his brother Artemiy, and his sister Amelia prepare *oladyi* (small thick pancakes) every Sunday morning.

SOUTH KOREA
Suh Eun helps hang clothes to dry, and folds them afterward.

MEXICO
Bosco waters the plants in the vegetable garden.

UGANDA

Daphine and her brother, mom, and housemaid usually eat dinner around ten at night at their big wooden table. They have *matoke* (a non-sweet banana) with groundnut (boiled and ground peanut) sauce, and milk to drink.

CAMBODIA

Viphou and his two brothers, mom, and dad usually eat dinner around seven in the evening at their metal kitchen table. They eat red curry soup, sweet fish with vegetables in a sweet-and-sour sauce, and end their meal with oranges.

This is how we eat dinner.

I eat dinner at _____, with my _____

_____.

I usually eat _____

_____ and drink _____.

COLOMBIA

Magdalem and her parents cook on a stove made of bricks. They spend many hours each week collecting firewood that they use for fuel.

TUNISIA

Karim and his family use a gas stove. The next thing they want to buy is a refrigerator.

ZIMBABWE

Maclean, his two brothers, Macdecide and Maxmillan, and his parents use wood for cooking in their outdoor stove made of bricks.

This is how we cook our food.

We use a _____ to cook our meals.

CAMBODIA
Kong Darung, his two brothers, and his mom cook their meals on a portable gas hot plate.

BRAZIL
Helena and her parents have a gas stove in their kitchen. They also own a microwave and a toaster oven.

This is what I do in the evening.

After dinner, I _____

_____ .

AUSTRALIA
Twyla plays with
Dandelion Willow Blue,
her pet bunny rabbit.

ISRAEL
Yaron practices guitar
with his younger
brother Raviv.

ITALY
Romeo works on model
cars with his dad.

CANADA
Avery and her sister
Sadie read their favorite
books in bed.

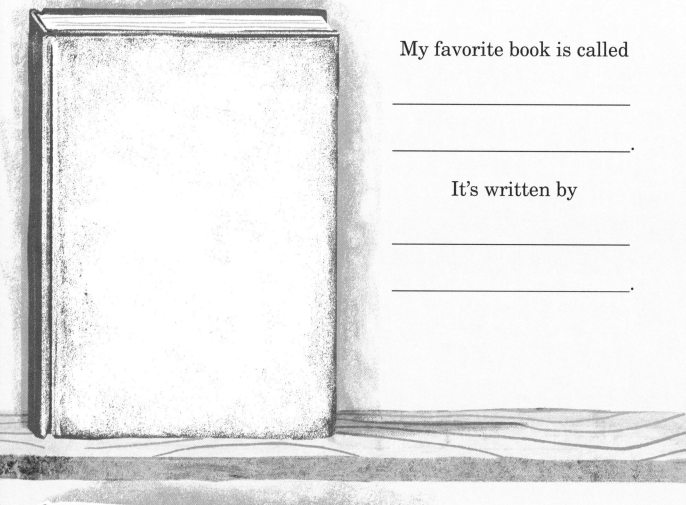

My favorite book is called

_____

_____.

It's written by

_____

_____.

JAPAN

Guri and Gura, by Rieko Nakagawa, is first in a series of books about twin field mice. In the first story, the mice discover a huge egg, and decide to make a gigantic cake.

SWEDEN

The Moomins and the Great Flood, by Tove Jansson, is the first in a series of nine books about the adventures of a family of hippopotamus-like creatures.

GHANA

Sosu's Call, by Meshack Asare, is a story of a boy who cannot walk, who warns his village of an approaching storm with his drumming.

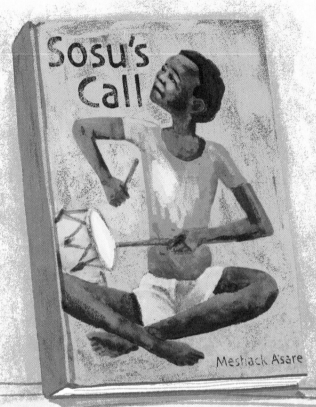

IRAN

Little Black Fish, by Samad Behrangi, is a story of a fish who is not afraid to swim out of his pool to discover the world that lies beyond.

URUGUAY

Ariadna sleeps next to her sister, who often climbs in bed with her because she doesn't like sleeping alone.

SPAIN

Miró sleeps between his mom and dad on their big bed. He goes to sleep before his parents, between eight and nine in the evening.

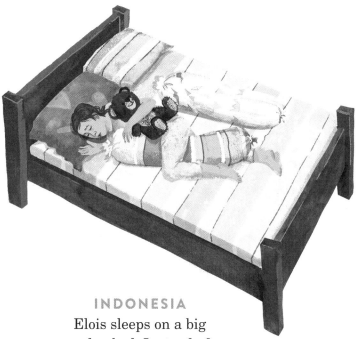

INDONESIA

Elois sleeps on a big wooden bed. Instead of a blanket, she uses a *guling* (a body pillow). She goes to bed at ten at night.

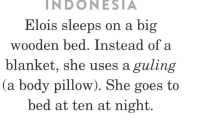

JAPAN

Nao sleeps on a futon on the floor, next to her older sister.

This is where I sleep.

My bedtime is _____. I sleep on _____

_____.

POSTCARDS

Use the postcards in the back of
this book to keep in touch with
friends and family who may live
far away from you, even if they
are looking up at the same moon.
Or, you can mail a postcard to
a pen-pal, or even the author
of this book. If you're looking
for some great resources for
communicating with other kids,
visit the website below.

www.thisishowwedoitbook.com

STICKERS

Use the stickers on the following
pages to decorate the postcards
or the interior pages!

MAP

Use the fold-out map to find the
countries referenced throughout
this book.

Draw something special
about your part of the world
inside each letter.

HELLO
from _____

What's your favorite dessert?
Draw a sweet that you'd want to
share with someone.

a
SWEET
for when we
MEET

Draw the place where you
live at sunset or sunrise.

GREETINGS FROM _____

Draw yourself on the left side,
and the person you're sending
the card to on the right side.

from
ME ⟶ YOU
to

THE WEATHER

IS BETTER

TOGETHER!

WHEN WE'RE

What season do you like best?
Draw yourself (and your friends
or family) doing an activity during
your favorite time of year.

I'VE BEEN
SEARCHING
for YOU!

Draw the place where you're
sending the postcard inside
the binoculars.

After I made the picture book, *This Is How We Do It*, I got an email from Jordyn, a Peace Corps volunteer, who had recently moved to the islands of Fiji and brought the book on her travels. The Fijian kids she was teaching loved the book so much they created their own versions of it, featuring drawings and descriptions of their lives. Jordyn emailed me photos of their beautiful books. It was heartwarming to see that the project had encouraged children to document their lives, and reach out to share them with me from so far away. They were the ones who inspired me to make this book.

To create this book, I contacted real families from dozens of countries from around the globe and asked them to take photographs and answer questions about specific parts of their day. I used their photos as reference materials to draw the illustrations in this book. In addition to those families, I also found many others on a website called Dollar Street, a wonderful project by Anna Rosling Rönnlund. The website is a free resource that features more than 500 families around the world, and catalogs a large variety of information about their lives, from the houses they live in, to the types of roofs and front doors they have, to their modes of transportation, to the toothbrushes they use. It's an incredible tool that gave me access to some families who would have been very difficult for me to find and speak with on my own. I was able to include people who live in remote places, don't speak English, or don't have access to the internet and digital cameras.

This Is How I Do It follows a day in the lives of 59 real kids, and gives you space to add what you do in your day, and see how it compares to the kids who share the world with you. As you flip through these pages, you'll find similarities and differences with the children you see. You may have the same kind of pet as Keza from Rwanda, but have a very different type of breakfast from Gayoon in South Korea. What Gayoon eats for breakfast may be a custom, something many people in that part of the world do in a similar way. Or it may be a personal choice, something that Gayoon likes to eat, but her friends and family don't particularly like. After all, each person in the world is unique.

This activity book can become a record of this moment in time, one that may be fun to read a few years from now. Maybe when you're older, and your hair has turned gray, you can revisit this day from your childhood the same way you might look at a photo album or open a time capsule.

I learned a lot about the lives of different children while making this book. It's been so fun corresponding with kids' families that I've included some postcards within these pages, hoping that the fun will continue: Will you make a drawing or write something, and send it my way? I'm hoping you'll use them to connect with one another, too.

Matt Lamothe

Use this map to mark the places
you've lived, the places you've visited,
and the places you want to go.

WHERE THE AUTHOR LIVES

Chicago, Illinois, United States

PLACES I'VE LIVED

_____
_____
_____
_____

PLACES MY FAMILY HAS LIVED

_____
_____
_____
_____
_____
_____